GRACE

PRAYERS FROM THE HEART OF
RECOVERY

BY

BRYAN NEVIN

RISHI

1

ISBN: 1522780297
ISBN 13: 9781522780298

Library of Congress Control Number:
2016901257

LCCN Imprint Name: Create Space
Independent Publishing Platform: North
Charleston, SC

This book is dedicated to everyone in recovery, in search of a better way of life.

Acknowledgments

Jimmy Courtney

I don't even know how to express my gratitude. The service of your mentorship is priceless. Your direction and fatherly love were a gift from God that I was longing for. The simplicity of Alcoholics Anonymous (AA) and the spiritual way of your life taught through your experiences started my journey. I am forever grateful.

Louise Nevin Rempe

For all the sleepless nights, for never giving up, for always believing in me and constantly praying, for never doubting, and for having endless faith and love.

Cathy M. Adcock

Your sense of humor, personality, and love help carry me through. You have been a rock and a support system.

Freehold Yoga Center

Devaki (Nina Sabatino), Omkar and Radha (Joe and Virgina DeOrio), Yogini (Linda Bennett) and the Center as a whole.

The spiritual guidance and love that radiate from all of you are a blessing. The teachings of spiritual enlightenment and lineage were an additional foundation to my spiritual journey. They enhanced my spiritual consciousness and elevated my awareness.

Mahan Rishi Singh Khalsa and
Nirbhe Kaur Khalsa

The authenticity of love and spirit that you both exemplify and teach is your gift to the world. It has been an honor for me to experience. The educational content and lineage of the Golden Chain that you live by is by spirit and for spirit. I am blessed to have had the opportunity to work with both of you. Your support and long-term friendship is something I cherish.

Jody Thompson

It's been a blessing to see you grow, pay it forward, and literally pull so many people from the depths of this affliction. Watching you progress from self to selflessness has been astounding. The service you give is nothing less than profound. It's a blessing to have you in my life.

Cole Porter, Tom Hale, Michael Holland, Fred Dunne, Steffan Manno, Frederick Johnson, Paul Horan, and Alice Grippa

These men and women, through their commitment and caring, paying it forward, and sharing their experience and time with me, have been a blessing. Without their support, none of this would be possible. Thank you for everything.

Introduction

I was one and a half to two years sober in AA, and my life had changed radically. I was placed on a new path, seeking a higher direction for my life. Prayer was new to me. In my morning meditation, I would write a daily prayer. I then sent the prayer as a text message to my friends, my network of people who were actively in recovery, seeking recovery, and changing their lives. It was a gesture of God's grace to me, and I just wanted to share it. The text messages were saved in my notes on an old phone. The prayers were dormant for many years, and I became inspired to share them, receiving the direction that these prayers should be turned into a book.

I have been blessed, and my purpose is to share my experience and share my hope. I am honored to have the opportunity to be alive and to contribute my experience with the world, and especially with those afflicted by alcoholism and drug addiction.

The Purpose of This Book

I wrote this to help people in recovery find the love that they long for, the light that has never existed, and God's grace that has been so violently opposed.

Twenty-five percent of the proceeds from this book will go toward helping youth and young adults who are struggling in recovery from alcoholism and drug addiction.

For every book that is sold, one book will be given to a newcomer in recovery.

God's

Riches

At

Christ's

Expense

Plunging into the depths of discouragement and becoming so preoccupied with our fears, we forget what God has done in our lives. We apply that selfish behavior, not even being aware of what we are doing. Taking our will back, wanting to figure everything out, when all we need to do is accept what is and give it to God. Much of this is easier said than done, but we need to ask Him, "Please, God, take my will, all of it. Give me the acceptance I am seeking to remove my fears. Help me trust in You."

Thank You. Amen.

Our strength and hope is being with God all the time.

By His grace I have been saved. God has blessed me with life. Our past gives wisdom for daily living, and only with God can I stand like a rock or a mountain. I know that the vision and power I receive from God are limitless. As far as spiritual things are concerned, I know I cannot see the road ahead or even the next step at times, but I must go on *one step at a time* and be with God. Please, God, carry me through that next step, and if need be, help me to ask You to carry me. Help me trust in You to be at my side and give light to what I am supposed to see and darkness to what I am to pass by.

Thank You. Amen.

Many books inform, but only one transforms. Perfect freedom only comes from trusting in God 110 percent.

While we acknowledge that not everyone is blessed with a bright outlook on life, we need to remember that joy is one of the gifts God promised. We need to resist any tendency to let sadness dominate our emotional life. No one can take joy from you but yourself. Joy is the fruit of the indwelling God. Please, God, dwell abundantly within me, so I may have Your joy overflowing. Help me look beyond my circumstances and encourage me by the vision of joy that awaits me. God, you are the foundation of my serenity.

Thank You. Amen.

Joy is a fruit of the spirit that's always in season. I believe that God is within and that I may enjoy eternal life with Him here and now.

To find peace and acquire serenity, I must not harbor disturbing thoughts. No matter what worries, fears, or resentments I may have, I must seek acceptance in all situations of my life. I must think constructively until calmness comes to me. Please, God, help me think positive and accept whatever You place on my path. Help me to build it up, rather than tearing down all You have done in my life. God, help me find that peace.

Thank You. Amen.

Only when I am calm and present can I act as a channel for God's spirit.

As fear and worry depart my life, the spirit comes in to take their place. Only when I am connected to the Great Spirit can I let go of my feelings and selfishness. Let my thoughts be the conscious contact to You, God. Please, God, remove my thinking mind for the day so I may be present with You. Sweep my life clean of any evil or impure thoughts that are not on Your plane so all I may receive is Your serenity and love. Please, God, influence my being with Your grace and serenity so I may be at peace with You.

Thank You. Amen.

The smallest example can be the biggest influence.

Quiet time, meditation, and prayer with God are essential in the walk of faith or the way of Spirit. This quiet time is a disconnect and is necessary in order to connect with God. Make time to meet with God. Keep in fit spirits. Start the day with God; otherwise there is no center, and all is off balance. Please, God, help me listen for the Spirit to guide me; keep me present and connected to You throughout the day so I may stay on Your path and not wind up lost on my own path alone.

Thank You. Amen.

Time spent with God is time well spent.

The future is in God's hands, and he knows best. With him I am being led in a very definite way. God rebuilds my life and directs it, not me. God is my guide. Please, God, help me live under your laws of love and peace as You would have me live. Help me depend on You, God.

Thank You. Amen.

For all I need is to be with God. If He is active in my life, I have nothing to worry about.

God will never give me a load greater than I can bear. This may not always seem true, though after we tend to look back and ask ourselves, smiling, "Where was my faith?" we find serenity and peace in all situations. Life is being with God, and this is where all true success lies. Please, God, strengthen Your presence in my life so peace and serenity are easily found when things are not going smooth and life is happening. May my spirit be filled with Your love at all times, good and bad.

Thank You. Amen.

To prepare for tomorrow, trust God today.

Sacrifice and suffering are of value to me today. Once I was in darkness; now I am in God's light. I may now accept pain and defeat as part of God's plan for my spiritual growth. When in pain or feeling defeated, I am being tested. The divine will is working in a way that is beyond my mind; I can trust it. Please, God, help me trust that Your plan is far better than anything I can ever imagine. Help me through the defeat and pain of life.

Thank You. Amen.

Once you become detached from external things, they do not own you any longer.

God always offers a fresh start. So put the old away and start new each day. God forgives all if you honestly try to live today the way He wants us to live. There is no way to enlightenment; enlightenment is the way. It is a principle of living. Please, God, help me not to spoil my day with worry and fear. Bring me to live with Your enlightenment, love, and peace.

Thank You. Amen.

We can start a new life each day or start the day over at any time.

Practice love. Lack of love will block the way. Try to see good in all, because it is there. The divine is everywhere. Am I open to realize this truth? Please, God, help me to see the divine in and around me, activate and accept more of Your love in my life. As I love, I will be loved.

Thank You. Amen.

The more love you can receive, the more you can give away. If you expect to be happy, healthy, fulfilled, and loved in life, then that's where you'll place your attention, and that's what you'll manifest.

All walls that are barriers in life can fall by your faith and God's power. There is no limit to what can be accomplished through His power. Anything can happen. Please, God, strengthen my faith day by day; make me a channel for You to pass through. Help me rely more and more on Your power and activate it in my life.

Thank You. Amen.

Great things happen if that faith in God's power is active.

I know that God cannot teach me anything if I am trusting a crutch. I must throw the crutch away, find the faith, and walk in God's spirit. God's strength and power will invigorate me to victory and have every day, by another day of sobriety. Please, God, help me to remain teachable and seek Your experience in my life, to grow abundantly in spirit with You and have another victory by keeping me sober today. God, set my recovery and life in spirit today.

Thank You. Amen.

A daily question is, What is my recovery set in? Am I set in spirit, or in abstinence? If it is spirit, it's all good. If it's abstinence, I am doomed.

Willingness and acceptance are the essence of change and all spiritual growth. Life is like a school in which we must learn to be taught. God is my teacher. I must trust in God. I must listen for God's direction. He does speak sometimes, though not out loud; most of the time it is a whisper. I must persist to listen and make God my habit. Please, God, help me listen so I may hear You and grow in Your light, love, happiness, and peace. Keep me seeking Your knowledge so I may help someone as hopeless as I once was.

Thank You. Amen.

God reveals himself to me in many ways daily. Open your mind.

Just to be near God, just to dwell in His presence is the longing I seek today. To be loved and able to feel that divine love within. Please, God, come to me and take away the loneliness. Help me not to isolate but seek to dwell in Your presence and keep me active in helping others so I will not get lost in self.

Thank You. Amen.

Within is the kingdom of serenity that can create all the prosperity that you could ever want.

Only with blind, trusting faith will the darkness be lightened and my prayers pierce the ears of God. Only the divine power of God will heal and help my human weaknesses. With God's power only a few steps away, I walk in His light. Please, God, keep me close to You. Keep me in Your joy. Keep me whole in my divine being as I walk on Your path.

Thank You. Amen.

Joy is divine, and so is suffering. There is much to be learned from both.

I must rely on God, trust in Him, depend on the divine power in all relationships and situations in my life. I must wait for His guidance in everything. Please, God, help me with patience, tolerance, and seeking your guidance. Don't let me mess up your accomplishments in my life. God, make all my decisions in my life.

Thank You. Amen.

With God all is possible.

The blissfulness of God is through life within. Linked to this knowledge, you can only grow in spirit as long as you constantly seek the presence of God in your life. Do not try to comprehend this with the mind; just accept it with the heart. Please, God, help me to accept and actively seek You in all areas of my life.

Thank You. Amen.

"Life is like riding a bike. To keep in balance, you need to keep it moving" *(Albert Einstein).*

In some situations, it is hard to find gratitude. With God's grace we have fought the hardest fight in life. Find the gratitude, because without it we can't experience God's grace working in our lives. Please, God, keep my gratitude focused on what You have done in my life.

Thank You. Amen.

God gives us the strength for the fight of life.

With God's help, there is no limit as long as faith is there. We must believe that He will conquer what we cannot. Please, God, take all obstacles out of my life so I may be closer to you.

Thank You. Amen.

If we allow God into our lives, life will be so much easier.

The power of living comes from God, not me or my own strength. God's power can be easily seen and experienced in our lives. We start to see this when we get rid of selfishness and do God's will. Please, God, help me overcome my own selfishness and clear the accumulation of my will so I may become more productive and do Your will.

Thank You. Amen.

Selfishness drains our spiritual power. Selflessness and service to others restores it.

By God's mercy and grace we have a second chance at life. God opens the door to a brand-new day, and with it comes God's strength if I choose to use it. Please, God, take all my fear and fill it with Your faith. Replenish my strength after each task so I may be of full benefit to You and my fellow man.

Thank You. Amen.

God is a god of second chances.

Nothing happens by mistake. God's master plan is far bigger than what I can comprehend. Please, God, help me to accept what is and stop trying to figure out what will come or what I should be doing. Help me to just be.

Thank You. Amen.

Be with God, and all will play out how it's supposed to.

God gives me all I need, not what I want. His love is more precious than anything I can see, feel, or buy. Please, God, help me find Your love within so I may be better at loving others.

Thank You. Amen.

God is the protective screen at all times.

Faith alone is the answer to my prayers and relationship with God. I never saw this truth until God blessed me and opened my mind, and I accepted certain things. Please, God, feed my faith because in that I find Your power, love, and peace. Keep me growing toward You. Help me be receptive to Your power.

Thank You. Amen.

Faith and compassion puts God's love into action.

I give all my life to You, God. You know my needs and fulfill them always. Grant me contentment as I strive for Your excellence each day. Help me to accept what is as dark as it may seem. Please, God, help my spiritual progress and program so I may better advance our relationship and become more of Your love, light, and peace.

Thank You. Amen.

Godliness with contentment is great gain.

God longs to lead us, as long as we are willing to be redirected and ask for His help. Please, God, direct my actions, my whole being, and my thinking. Surround me with Your love. You know what is best for me. You truly know my best interest even when it does not seem so. I trust in You, God. You know the way.

Thank You. Amen.

A man's heart plans his way, but God directs his steps.

God is my helper. God is with me, controlling all, so why worry? Where is my faith? At times it can be hard to find; even believing it is there can be difficult. Please, God, take my worries, calm me, and let nothing upset me. Please, let no material things control or choke out my spiritual life.

Thank You. Amen.

Anything that keeps you from growing is never worth defending.

When things are going smoothly, it is easy to find gratitude. When things are not, it is important to look extra hard for it. Please, God, help me find gratitude for all You have done in my life, for keeping me healthy and by Your side. Thank You for never giving up on me.

Thank You. Amen.

Saying "thank You" to God is a daily practice that is absolutely necessary.

"The ultimate measure of a man is not where he stands in moments of comfort and convenience, but where he stands at times of challenge and controversy" (Martin Luther King Jr.).

Count the blessings. Do I see the whole picture or only what I choose to see? God has blessed all abundantly in many ways. Please, God, help me see this truth, so I may have Your acceptance in all situations in my life. Help me handle life or whatever You place on my path.

Thank You. Amen.

God does not give us anything we can't handle.

You can find God's peace if you choose to seek it. No matter what you have gone through or done, God will make His peace available. There is perfect understanding when we leave it all to God. Please, God, help me give and leave all burdens to You.

Thank You. Amen.

True peace is the presence of God.

It does not matter what you have done. No one can fall beyond the reach of God's forgiveness and love. The broken spirit is what God wants so he can remold it to its original beauty.

Thank You, God, for healing my spirit. Amen.

Is life feeling too big to handle? There may not be easy answers to the challenges you are facing. But God promises that if we ask for wisdom, He will grant it. If we ask Him to take all our burdens, He will take them. If you seek Him, He will grant all to you. You do not have to face any overwhelming challenges of life alone.

Thank You, God. Amen.

Acknowledge God, and He shall direct
your path. I know who holds the future,
and I know who holds my hand. With
God things do not just happen.
Everything is planned by Him. Please,
God, help me to see this truth and take
off my blinders so I may see Your path
and the light.

Thank You. Amen.

A mere happening may be God's design.

God and AA have given us a do-over, another chance at life, a provision to repair or restore what has been broken or damaged by our will. God has provided a method of restoration. If we ask Him for help, if we seek Him, He will forgive us and cleanse us from all unrighteousness. This is contingent on our relationship with Him.

Thank You. Amen.

Please, God, keep me in fit spiritual condition and close to You.

God, give me Your love. Open my heart abundantly. Help me seek You in my life so I may be at peace with myself and with You all the time. God, I ask this so I may do Your work effectively and share what You have already done for me.

Thank You. Amen.

To face life's many challenges and overcome each test, God tells us to take the time to stop, pray, breathe, and meditate. Please, God, help me take the time I need to give to You for my sanity.

Thank You. Amen.

To make the most of your time, take time to meditate, pray, and thank God.

God's love guides, warms, and shows the way. We are always put to His test, but He does not give us anything we cannot overcome. Please, God, give me your guidance, strength, and love today.

Thank You. Amen.

God, put the people in my life that belong and remove those that don't. Please, God, open the doors that need to be opened and close the doors that need to be closed.

Thank You. Amen.

All we need to do is ask, take action, and believe.

I have a companion. A wonderful guide, a comfort, a friend, never failing. Please, God, help me call on You when I need guidance, a friend, or some comfort. I pray that You fill my life with Your friendship and love so that our relationship can be brought to a higher plane.

Thank You. Amen.

To be with God is to be present with thyself.

Wholeness means that all parts work together as one. God's spirit heals. He is the one healing, but we have to work hard to improve our connection with Him. Please, God, help me to work on my spiritual wholeness and connection with You.

Thank You. Amen.

To become whole, keep yielding to the spirit of God.

God has given us gifts to serve Him. We will lose out if we fail to give Him our best. Give your best to God, and He will give himself to you. We are at our best when we serve God by serving others and do His work. Please, God, help me serve You and do Your work throughout the day so I may not be caught up in self.

Thank You. Amen.

God provides just what we need, just when we need it. He is constantly caring for us and seeking the best for us. He always cares and is never changing. He is constant love. Please, God, keep giving me what I need and fill my heart with Your loving care.

Thank You. Amen.

What God promises, God will provide. Have faith.

Spirit of God, help me to be a man or woman of peace and Your love. Give me new and healthy desires. Take away all that does not belong. Change all that needs to be changed. Clear my mind so I may be at peace and bliss with You.

Thank You. Amen.

No change is a cause for alarm. All change is from God.

God's goodness and grace saved me.
Please, God, keep this truth in my sight.
I pray that You fill me with more of Your
goodness and grace. Keep saving me
from self, remove self, and fill me with
spirit.

Thank You. Amen.

God, bless me through the day. Keep me safe and close to you. Show me Your love. Help me do Your work.

Thank You. Amen.

God will bring you into His light if you ask Him to. God's power is all around us. We see the power in our own lives if we ask Him to help us see it. We feel God's power through His love for us. Please, God, help me see and feel Your power in my life.

Thank You. Amen.

Good exercise for the heart is to bend down and help another person up. This is our high spot in life. If we do not share what was so freely given, we will lose it. Please, God, help me give away all that You have given me so I may live closer to You.

Thank You. Amen.

God provides strength in His own way through the eyes of faith. We see His strength working in our own lives. Please, God, open my eyes so I may see Your strength. Take away my worry and fear, so I may always see that You are near.

Thank You. Amen.

Those who let God provide will be satisfied.

God, at this time of a new year starting, I look back and clearly see all You have done in my life. I pray that You keep bringing me closer to You. Keep filling my life with Your loving blessings so I may share them and do Your work.

Thank You. Amen.

God comes to live with us so we can live with Him.

God is my hope. My faith comes from what He has done in my life and from past experience. I pray, please, God, build my faith so I may grow with you abundantly. Keep fresh with me where I was and how easy it would be to go back instead of forward. Keep all that You have done clearly in front of me and on my mind.

Thank You. Amen.

God's strength is made perfect in weakness. God finds the strength in the weak, removes the weakness, and replenishes it with love. Please, God, fill me with Your strength in times of weakness, so I am guided by Your love and presence.

Thank You. Amen.

Life is a battle, but it is also a blessing. God is here with us. We who have endured self-conflicting suffering can see the blessings clearly if we choose to. Please, God, keep Your blessings clear, help me preserve them with Your compassion, and root me in Your rich and life-filled soil, so I may abundantly grow with You.

Thank You. Amen.

God provides the power we need.

The law of the spirit of God has made me free from death and has given me a blessed, peaceful life. Thank You, God, for entering my being when You did and filling me with Your love and life. Please, God, keep my gratitude high and keep Your blessings plentiful. I pray not just for me but for all in and around my life.

Thank You. Amen.

Pursuing God in prayer and meditation is cause and effect. We do it because it draws us closer to God in our relationship. The roots of stability come from being grounded in the relationship with God. Please, God, help me to continually seek Your presence in my life.

Thank You. Amen.

God will help us face whatever comes our way and draw us closer to Him.

God's faithful care will extend to every day of the new year if we allow God to work in and through our lives. That is, choosing to do His will, not mine. God, how can I serve You? Please, God, show me through this new year of life how I can do Your work and keep my gratitude high.

Thank You. Amen.

God holds the future in His hands, and all will play out perfectly.

Growth and change do not happen all at once but gradually, day by day. It begins with a willingness to constantly seek God's love in our lives and work toward a relationship with Him. Search, and you will surely find treasures to enrich the spirit, mind, and body. Please, God, help me to seek and find You.

Thank You. Amen.

Rich treasures of God's truth are waiting to be discovered.

We do not need to walk the path of life alone anymore. We did for long enough. We have access to God wherever we go and in all situations. Please, God, help me access Your being in my life throughout the day, so I may be at peace with You.

Thank You. Amen.

God's presence brings great comfort.

God, widen my world. Help me to be a part of your work. Give me eyes to see as You see, hands to serve You and others, and a heart to share Your love. You have blessed me with all this, but I seek and ask for it in abundance.

God, hear my prayer.

Thank You. Amen.

If you look through the eyes of God, you will see the blessings all around.

Service to God now is what counts. Thy will. How may I serve God? We need to work for God here and now, not later. Please, God, help me serve You. Bring me to Your service level so You may save others the way You saved me.

Thank You. Amen.

If we do God's work here, we will live with God forever.

I suffered trouble to the point of chains, but God was the only one that broke the chains and freed me from self He brought me to live with Him at peace. Please, God, keep me close to You, keep me free from the chains. Fill me with Your love so I may pass it on as You did to me.

Thank You. Amen.

God is always right next to us. Do I choose to use Him?

God, I marvel at the wonders You have done with my life and with my being. Please, God, heal and help me to be fit to receive Your love, power, and blessings.

Thank You. Amen.

God does not change; He is always the same (love). Place your life in God's hands, and have no worries.

God gave me the acceptance to recognize something of lasting value, my relationship with Him and my life. In even our most ordinary tasks, I need to see God's work and meaning in my life. Please, God, help me see Your purpose and path in my life.

Thank You. Amen.

We need faith.

Whatever difficulties You have for me throughout life, help me to accept them. In all situations, there is growth or advancement toward God. Please, God, fill me with Your peace even in difficulties; help me to make the right choices and decisions.

Thank You for all my experiences.
Amen.

God is always with us.

When we cling to the one who has all power and knowledge, we are in good hands. Regardless of where He leads, many things about tomorrow I don't seem to understand. I know who holds tomorrow, and I know who holds my hand. Please, God, help me stay with You in the present day. Give me Your faith and love.

Thank You. Amen.

Never be afraid to entrust the unknown future to the all-knowing God.

Fix my eyes on You, God. You point the way. Your spirit is alive, and I have no worries. I want You and Your principles at all times throughout the day. Please, God, help me seek You abundantly and bless all that are a part of my life.

Thank You. Amen.

Follow God, and it all works out.

Good example has more value than good advice. Acting in love, purity, spirit, and faith is God's presence within you. Seek God's will, and love, purity, spirit, and faith will be in abundance. Please, God, help me to live a godly life of love, purity, spirit, and faith.

Thank You. Amen.

Seek God in all you do. Become a pilgrim of God who only needs strength and guidance for the day.

God, I ask that you help me see all the gifts You have given me in the past year. Please help me to find the gratitude that You deserve in abundance. Take off the blinders so I may see the light of You within me.

Please help in this time of need.

Thank You. Amen.

To renew your love for God, review God's love for you. This will help us to grow in our faith and belief. To be thankful to know the love of God, we must ground ourselves in God's love. Please, God, ground me in Your love today.

Thank You. Amen.

Every obstacle that comes along is an opportunity to change and grow. God only puts in front of us what He knows we can handle. Please, God, help me see this truth.

Thank You. Amen.

The spirit is God's power supply that is alive in every one of us. The question is, how do we tap into it? We develop spiritually through God. This dependence on God through the work of the spirit in our lives is at the core of our walk with God. If we think we become like God by our own efforts, we are fooling ourselves. Please, God, help me grow at Your core spiritually.

Thank You. Amen.

God, I know I cannot save myself. I need You as my savior. I want to live with You all the time. You are the way to love, light, life, and happiness. Please, God, fill my life with Your light so all may see how remarkable You are.

Thank You. Amen.

The greatest gift that has ever been given is God. This gift can be yours if you will believe. Be willing and trust in Him, receive a new life, and live at peace with yourself. Please, God, help me trust that all is good with You.

Thank You. Amen.

God can take all problems only if we ask Him to and do not try to take them back and fix them ourselves. God can defeat all as long as we ask and have faith. Please, God, build my faith abundantly so I may not have to worry about what I can't handle.

Thank You. Amen.

The only thing that can separate me from God is myself. Nothing can separate me from God's love but self. God's never-failing love and presence is always there. Do I choose to see it? That is the question. Please, God, help me to always seek You and see Your presence in all areas of my life.

Thank You. Amen.

While I need help and should not live in isolation, I ask You to come into my heart. It is not outside sources that provide true happiness. This comes from within, from the relationship I have with God, from letting God be at home in my heart. Please, God, dwell within my heart and be at my side throughout the day. Help me see Your truth so I may be truly happy.

Thank You. Amen.

If a troubled world gets you down, look up to God.

About the Author

Bryan has a miraculous story of surviving and conquering the demons in his life overcoming the web of mental viruses and addictions.

At eleven years old, he turned down the long road of substance abuse, starting with alcohol. He progressed to marijuana and hallucinogens. At thirteen years old, he began his criminal career. His journey took him to nine rehabs, several detox centers, and dozens of confinements in jails. This left a wreckage—of broken relationships, hurt family members, and a criminal background that still haunts him today. Bryan ended with a heroin addiction that lasted nine years. Having lost everything from his addiction, including his dignity, he was broken. God literally picked him up from the depths and gave him a newfound life and a second chance.

By the grace of God, Bryan is now over eight years clean and sober, enjoying a life of service, structured recovery, and healthy living. God separated Bryan from alcohol and drugs on September 7 of 2007. Bryan lives in New Jersey and works in the consulting industry for sustainable products. His passion is working with youth and young adults in sharing his experience, strength, hope, and knowledge about the devastating consequences of making poor choices.

His future goals include expanding his outreach to parents and family since he believes the family dynamic within addiction is most important.

Today

Bryan has a passion for motivating, encouraging, and inspiring others.

He is also a certified Sivananda and Kundalini yoga instructor. He practices meditation and believes it is an essential element to his recovery, contentment, and healthy lifestyle.

Bryan's success personally and through recovery is miraculous in many ways.

Connect with Bryan Nevin

Speaking Engagements/Workshops
Targeting:

- Addictive disorders in adults and youth.
- Family dynamics in addiction.
- Relapse prevention.
- Recovery based yoga and meditation.

"Experience is the best teacher"

bryan.nevin@gmail.com

About the Author

Bryan has a miraculous story of surviving and conquering the demons in his life overcoming the web of mental viruses and addictions.

At eleven years old, he turned down the long road of substance abuse, starting with alcohol. He progressed to marijuana and hallucinogens. At thirteen years old, he began his criminal career. His journey took him to nine rehabs, several detox centers, and dozens of confinements in jails. This left a wreckage—of broken relationships, hurt family members, and a criminal background that still haunts him today. Bryan ended with a heroin addiction that lasted nine years. Having lost everything from his addiction, including his dignity, he was broken. God literally picked him up from the depths and gave him a newfound life and a second chance.

By the grace of God, Bryan is now over eight years clean and sober, enjoying a life of service, structured recovery, and healthy living. God separated Bryan from alcohol and drugs on September 7 of 2007. Bryan lives in New Jersey and works in the consulting industry for sustainable products. His passion is working with youth and young adults in sharing his experience, strength, hope, and knowledge about the devastating consequences of making poor choices.

His future goals include expanding his outreach to parents and family since he believes the family dynamic within addiction is most important.

Photos taken by Cathy Adcock
Art and formatting done by Bryan Nevin

29356788R00061

Made in the USA
Middletown, DE
16 February 2016